My Daily Diet: Fruits

On My Plate

On My Plate

My Daily Diet: Fruits

Rosa Waters

Mason Crest

Mason Crest
450 Parkway Drive, Suite D
Broomall, PA 19008
www.masoncrest.com

Printed and bound in the United States of America.

First printing
9 8 7 6 5 4 3 2 1

Series ISBN: 978-1-4222-3094-7
ISBN: 978-1-4222-3097-8
ebook ISBN: 978-1-4222-8788-0

Library of Congress Cataloging-in-Publication Data

Waters, Rosa, 1957- author.
  My daily diet : fruits / Rosa Waters.
      pages cm. — (On my plate)
  Audience: Age 9+
  Audience: Grade 4 to 6.
  Includes bibliographical references and index.
  ISBN 978-1-4222-3097-8 (hardback) — ISBN 978-1-4222-3094-7 (series) — ISBN 978-
1-4222-8788-0 (ebook) 1. Fruit in human nutrition—Juvenile literature. 2. Fruit—Juvenile
literature. I. Title.
  QP144.F78W38 2015
  613.2—dc23
                                        2014010565

Contents

KEY ICONS TO LOOK FOR:

Text-Dependent Questions: These questions send the reader back to the text for more careful attention to the evidence presented there.

Words to Understand: These words with their easy-to-understand definitions will increase the reader's understanding of the text, while building vocabulary skills.

Series Glossary of Key Terms: This back-of-the book glossary contains terminology used throughout this series. Words found here increase the reader's ability to read and comprehend higher-level books and articles in this field.

Research Projects: Readers are pointed toward areas of further inquiry connected to each chapter. Suggestions are provided for projects that encourage deeper research and analysis.

Sidebars: This boxed material within the main text allows readers to build knowledge, gain insights, explore possibilities, and broaden their perspectives by weaving together additional information to provide realistic and holistic perspectives.

Introduction

Most of us would agree that building healthy bodies and minds is a critical component of future success in school, work, and life. Providing our bodies with adequate and healthy nutrition in childhood sets the stage for both optimal learning and healthy habits in adulthood. Research suggests that the epidemic of overweight and obesity in young children leads to a large medical and financial burden, both for individuals and society. Children who are overweight and obese are more likely to become overweight or obese adults, and they are also at increased risk for a range of diseases.

Developing healthy eating and fitness habits in childhood is one of the most important gifts we can all provide to children in our homes and workplaces—but as any parent can attest, this is not always an easy task! Children are surrounded with both healthy and unhealthy eating options in their homes, schools, and in every restaurant or store they visit. Glossy marketing of food and meals is ubiquitous in media of all types, impacting both children's and adults' eating choices. As a result of the multiple influences on eating choices, from infancy through adulthood, we all benefit from additional support in making healthy choices.

Just as eating and fitness can become habits in adulthood, personal decision-making in childhood is critical to developing healthy habits. Providing healthy options and examples are a starting point, which can support children's healthy habits, but children also benefit from understanding the rationale for eating reasonable portions of healthy foods. Parents, teachers, and others often communicate messages through their words and actions—but books can provide more detailed information and pictures.

Building on this need for developing informed consumers, the ON MY PLATE series provides elementary school children with an informative yet fun introduction to their eating options. Beginning with an introduction to the five food groups, children can learn about what they ideally will have on their own plate and in their mouths. Tips are provided for choosing healthy snacks. And children will understand the importance of eating a range of foods. These books empower our children to make healthy decisions for themselves.

An additional benefit of this series may be the trickle-up effect for parents. Even if we all *know* the importance of making healthy choices for meals and snacks, there's nothing like a child *reminding us* why this is important. When our children start citing the long-term consequences of our dietary choices, we tend to listen!

Here's to developing healthy eating habits today!

Lisa Albers Prock, MD, MPH
Developmental Behavioral Pediatrician, Boston Children's Hospital
Assistant Professor, Harvard Medical School

WORDS TO UNDERSTAND

digestive system: The parts of your body that help take in food and get your body what it needs from the things you eat.

specialize: To focus on a smaller number of things.

factory: A business where different things are made, including different foods.

warehouse: A building used to keep food while it's being moved from one place to another.

products: The things people buy and sell.

produce: Fruits and vegetables.

public: Open to everyone.

Chapter 1

Where Does Fruit Come From?

When you grab an apple before school, that apple has a long history. It has likely traveled a long way to get to you and been passed through many people's hands. Once you eat it, the apple's story isn't over yet either. Your *digestive system* kicks in, turning that apple into fuel that will keep your body going.

Every fruit (and every other food, for that matter) has a story. If you follow that story back to its beginning, you may find out some surprising things about that piece of fruit you're about to bite into.

FARMS

All fruit starts out on a farm. These days, farms tend to *specialize* in one or two crops. One farm might just grow apples. Another grows oranges. A third grows strawberries. Fruit farms tend to be very large, growing rows and rows of fruit.

You can find fruit farms all over the world. Some of the fruit people eat in North

Many fruits are grown on a farm like this one and then shipped all over the world for people to eat. Many fruits will only grow in a certain kind of climate.

America comes from North American farms. Oranges, for example, often come from the state of Florida. Apples are grown in Washington State and New York State, among other places.

Other fruits travel a long way to get to you. Bananas, mangos, and pineapples are fruits that don't grow very well in most places in North America. Bananas, for example, are mostly grown in India, Latin America, and the Philippines. They need a hot place to grow.

Fruits grow on plants, which grow in the ground on farms. Different sorts of fruits

MAKE CONNECTIONS

Some fruit is organic and some is not. Organic means that farmers didn't use chemicals to grow their produce. Farmers often use chemicals to kill bugs and help their plants grow bigger. Many people don't want to eat fruit and other foods that have been grown with chemicals, though. Chemicals can make farmworkers sick, pollute the soil and water and kill animals, and even make people who eat the food sick. Grocery stores often have a section of fruits and vegetables that are all organic.

MAKE CONNECTIONS

Another local fruit option is to go to the farm and pick it yourself! Areas that are close to the countryside often have a few farms that let people visit and pick the fruit they're growing. Pick-your-own farms offer apples, pumpkins, berries, peaches, and other fruits and vegetables.

grow on different sorts of plants. Berries, like blueberries and raspberries, grow on bushes. Mangos, apples, peaches, oranges, lemons, and many more of the larger fruits grow on trees. Strawberries grow on small plants that grow low to the ground. Grapes and melons grow on vines.

All fruit has one thing in common—they all come from the earth. Every fruit you've ever eaten has grown in the ground. In fact, all of the food we eat comes from the earth. Dirt, sunlight, and water have all worked together to create the fruit we eat.

Farmers and farmworkers also have parts to play in all the fruit we eat. Farmers choose what fruit to grow, how to grow it, and how to harvest it. Farmworkers do the hard work of taking care of the fruit plants and picking the fruit when it's ready. On very large farms, hundreds of farmworkers may spend hours and hours every day picking fruit during the harvest season. Then, once the fruit is picked, it's ready for the next step in its journey to your table.

FACTORIES AND WAREHOUSES

After it leaves the farm, fruit generally gets shipped to either a **factory** or a **warehouse**. Fresh fruit like a peach may get shipped right to a warehouse. All the peaches that arrive at the warehouse are organized based on where they will end up after they leave.

A lot of fruit is made into other **products**, not just eaten fresh. Jam and jelly, juice, and dried fruit are all products made from fresh fruit that have gone through a few extra steps before they get to you. Most of that fruit is shipped from farms to factories.

Factories make some fruit into jam. Factory workers mix sugar and some other ingredients into the fruit and heat it all up. Machines pour the jam into cans and seal them, and then they're ready to head out of the factory.

Jam is just one product that is made out of fruit. Some fruit is pressed into juice. Other fruit is dried out and packaged as raisins, dried apples, dried apricots, and other dried fruit. Some fresh fruit is cut up in factories and mixed together to make fresh fruit salads.

STORES

The fruit and fruit products then make their way from the factories and warehouses to grocery stores. Trucks, trains, airplanes, and boats all bring the fruit to their final destinations. Sometimes more than one kind of transportation is involved in shipping the fruit.

RESEARCH PROJECT

Choose a fruit you enjoy eating. Then draw a diagram of its story, starting with the farm where it grew. Check the label on the fruit to find out where it came from. Go to your grocery store or the market where you bought the fruit and ask the people there to tell you if they know where the fruit came from. Where was it grown? Did it go to a warehouse? Where was the warehouse? Did it travel on a truck or a plane? Find out as much as you can by asking questions. Then use the Internet to fill in any gaps in your fruit's story. Draw a picture for each step of the story. Label each step's picture and then make an arrow that leads to the next step.

If a banana grown in Ecuador has to get to a town outside Montreal in Canada, lots of different kinds of transportation might be used. First, the bananas may travel by truck from the banana warehouse to the airport. Then the bananas are loaded on planes and flown to Montreal. Next the bananas are unloaded and put back on trucks or maybe on a train to get to the town outside the city. Finally, the bananas are unloaded at the grocery store and put on the store's shelves.

This is what happens all around the world, bringing fruit to stores. And now here's where you come in. You or your family takes a look at all the fruit available in the store. You buy what you like to eat and what looks good. Then you take it home and eat it.

The next time you're at the grocery store, take a look at all the fruit that's there. Lots of that fruit has a label or a sign telling you where it comes from. See if you can spot all the places around the world the fruit has traveled from.

You can also think about all the people involved in getting that fruit from the farm to you. Farmers and farmworkers cared for the fruit plants, and then they picked the fruit and sent it to warehouses and factories. Other workers loaded the fruit on trucks, trains, planes, or ships. Truck drivers, airplane and ship captains, airport workers, train conductors, and other workers all helped transport the fruit. Grocery store workers unloaded the fruit and put it on shelves.

That's a lot of people to get you one banana!

LOCAL FRUIT

Most of the fruit we eat is grown on big farms, shipped to factories and warehouses, and sold at big grocery stores. Some fruit, however, travels a different and shorter path.

Many people shop at farmers' markets. They buy fruits and vegetables directly from farmers who grew the food. The farmers live nearby; they grow the food nearby. Then the farmers bring it to the market where they all get together once or more a week and sell to people who want fresh fruits and vegetables.

TEXT-DEPENDENT QUESTIONS

1. This chapter says that fruit has a story. What does the chapter say is the first step in a fruit's story?

2. What does this chapter say is the thing that all fruits have in common?

3. Describe some of the things this chapter says could happen to fruit at a factory.

4. What does it mean if fruit is organic?

5. What is local food?

Local food can also come from people's own gardens. Lots of people grow gardens in their yards or on their porches and decks. Some people have garden plots in a community garden, where lots of people garden together because they don't have space by their homes.

In a garden, you can grow *produce* yourself and then bring it right home. Depending on where you live, you can grow strawberries, blueberries, raspberries, melons, grapes, and other fruits.

Apple trees, fig trees, lemon trees, and other fruit trees all produce fruit you can pick and bring home! Some people own fruit trees right in their own yards. Other fruit trees grow in *public* spaces. They belong to the city or town.

The journey from plant to plate is a lot shorter for local food. Your fruit doesn't have to be picked thousands of miles away. No one has to ship it to you, and you don't have to go to the grocery store to buy it. Food that has gone on such a short journey is called local food. And growing your own fruit is as local as you can get!

Lots of people eat local because they don't like the story behind fruit that is grown on huge farms and shipped a long distance. Farmworkers who work on big farms are often not treated very well, and they don't make much money. Shipping fruit across the world uses up a lot of gas and contributes to pollution. Buying or growing local food can help avoid some of these problems.

No matter where it comes from, though, fruit is part of a healthy diet. You should eat fruit every day to stay healthy and grow up strong. Besides, fruit is not only healthy—it's delicious!

WORDS TO UNDERSTAND

substances: The materials or things that make something.

organs: Parts of your body made to do a certain task such as your heart pumping blood or your lungs breathing.

tissues: The materials (skin and muscle and bone) living things are made of.

digest: The way your body breaks down food into the nutrients you need.

cancers: A disease that causes harmful cells in the body to grow, divide, and spread. Cancer can affect different parts of the body.

diabetes: A disease in which patients have too much of a certain type of sugar (called glucose) in their blood because their bodies can't make enough insulin, which keeps blood sugar normal.

stroke: A health problem caused by a blocked or broken blood vessel in the brain.

cataracts: A problem with the eyes that causes them to get cloudy and sight to become blurry.

obesity: Having too much body fat and being overweight. Not all overweight people are obese, but all obese people are overweight.

asthma: A health problem that can make breathing more difficult. Asthma can also cause coughing, wheezing, or tightness in the chest.

high blood pressure: A health problem caused by too much blood pumping through veins that are too small. The force of the blood against the walls of the veins can cause other health issues, such as problems with the heart.

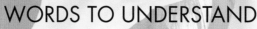

Chapter 2

Why Do I Need to Eat Fruits Every Day?

"**A**n apple a day keeps the doctor away" is a famous expression. The saying has some truth to it—eating fruit every day will help keep you healthy. You don't have to always eat an apple, but you should eat some kind of fruit every day! They're full of nutrients.

WHAT ARE NUTRIENTS?

Nutrients are the *substances* inside foods that make food good for you. They are in all the foods we eat. But you won't see the nutrients if you cut up your food into tiny pieces on your plate. Nutrients are even smaller than that.

Even though nutrients are so tiny, they are very important to people's health. People

The potassium in bananas helps your cells work the way they should. It also helps lower blood pressure, and it might reduce the risk of having a stroke when you get older.

need the right balance of nutrients to stay healthy. Nutrients keep the body working right, from your brain to your muscles to your blood.

Vitamins and minerals are two kinds of nutrients in food. Vitamins are named with letters. They include vitamins A, B, C, D, E, and K. Minerals include calcium, potassium, magnesium, iron, and others. Each one of those vitamins and minerals helps out your body in a slightly different way. Vitamins and minerals are called micronutrients. People need to eat them in tiny amounts every day.

People also need to eat macronutrients. We need larger amounts of macronutrients every day than we do micronutrients. The macronutrients we need are protein, carbohydrates, and fat. Protein keeps muscles strong and healthy. It helps young people grow and develop. Carbohydrates are divided into three types: sugar, starch, and fiber. Carbohydrates provide the body with a lot of energy. They give your body fuel, sort of like the gas people pump into their cars. The third kind of carbohydrate, fiber, keeps the digestive system moving and healthy. People also need certain kinds of fats (but not too much of certain kinds) to store energy and protect the body's *organs*.

MAKE CONNECTIONS

You don't need to keep track of every single nutrient you eat. As long as you eat a variety of fruit, you'll be getting the benefits of all the nutrients fruit have. If in doubt, try and eat a rainbow of fruits (and vegetables). Each color of fruit helps keep you healthy in a slightly different way, based on what's in those fruits.

- Red and pink: Keeps the heart healthy, and may protect against cancer. Eat apples, strawberries, red grapes, and pink grapefruit.
- Orange and yellow: Keeps eyes and skin healthy and helps you see better. Oranges, pineapples, mangoes, and lemons all fall in this category.
- Green: Green fruits protect the eyes, protect against cancer, and they build strong bones. Green fruits include green grapes and kiwi.
- Blue and purple: Blue fruits may improve memory and thinking and may also reduce cancer, heart disease, and stroke. Blueberries, blackberries, and purple grapes count as blue.
- Brown and white: Lower cholesterol and blood pressure, help the immune system, and keep the digestive system healthy. Bananas and lychees fall in this category.

One of the reasons food is healthy or not is based on how many nutrients it has. A food with lots of good nutrients is usually considered to be healthy. A food without many good nutrients or too much of some like sugar and sodium (salt) is not as healthy. Fruits definitely falls into the healthy category!

FRUIT NUTRIENTS

Fruit contains plenty of good nutrients. That's why fruits are so healthy. Fruit have lots of different nutrients, but they are very high in certain ones.

Several fruits have a lot of potassium. Eating foods with potassium is tied to having a healthy blood pressure. Good sources of potassium include bananas and prunes.

Fruits also have lots of vitamins in them. They're especially high in two—vitamins A and C. Vitamin A protects your skin and eyes. Good fruit sources of vitamin A include melons and apricots. Many fruits also have lots of vitamin C. Vitamin C helps keep body *tissues* healthy. It helps cuts heal and keeps your gums and teeth healthy. Citrus, kiwis, strawberries, and mangoes all have high levels of vitamin C.

All fruits also contain some dietary fiber. People don't actually digest fiber, but fiber is still an important part of health. Fiber keeps your digestive system moving. Scientists think it may help keep your heart healthy. Fiber also fills you up. You don't have to eat so much to feel full when you eat foods with fiber. Not overeating helps you keep from getting too heavy.

Fruit also has sugar. Sugar is a type of carbohydrate, and too much of it can be bad for you. Fruit and candy aren't the same thing, even though they both have sugar. One candy bar will pack in a ton of sugar. One apple will have much less, but you'll be fuller after you

Raw, edible weight portion.
Percent Daily Values (%DV) are based on a 2,000 calorie diet.

Fruits Serving Size (gram weight/ounce weight)	Calories	Calories from Fat	Total Fat g / %DV	Sodium mg / %DV	Potassium mg / %DV	Total Carbohydrate g / %DV	Dietary Fiber g / %DV	Sugars g	Protein g	Vitamin A %DV	Vitamin C %DV	Calcium %DV	Iron %DV
Apple 1 large (242 g/8 oz)	130	0	0 / 0	0 / 0	260 / 7	34 / 11	5 / 20	25g	1g	2%	8%	2%	2%
Avocado California, 1/5 medium (30 g/1.1 oz)	50	35	4.5 / 7	0 / 0	140 / 4	3 / 1	1 / 4	0g	1g	0%	4%	0%	2%
Banana 1 medium (126 g/4.5 oz)	110	0	0 / 0	0 / 0	450 / 13	30 / 10	3 / 12	19g	1g	2%	15%	0%	2%
Cantaloupe 1/4 medium (134 g/4.8 oz)	50	0	0 / 0	20 / 1	240 / 7	12 / 4	1 / 4	11g	1g	120%	80%	2%	2%
Grapefruit 1/2 medium (154 g/5.5 oz)	60	0	0 / 0	0 / 0	160 / 5	15 / 5	2 / 8	11g	1g	35%	100%	4%	0%
Grapes 3/4 cup (126 g/4.5 oz)	90	0	0 / 0	15 / 1	240 / 7	23 / 8	1 / 4	20g	0g	0%	2%	2%	0%
Honeydew Melon 1/10 medium melon (134 g/4.8 oz)	50	0	0 / 0	30 / 1	210 / 6	12 / 4	1 / 4	11g	1g	2%	45%	2%	2%
Kiwifruit 2 medium (148 g/5.3 oz)	90	10	1 / 2	0 / 0	450 / 13	20 / 7	4 / 16	13g	1g	2%	240%	4%	2%
Lemon 1 medium (58 g/2.1 oz)	15	0	0 / 0	0 / 0	75 / 2	5 / 2	2 / 8	2g	0g	0%	40%	2%	0%
Lime 1 medium (67 g/2.4 oz)	20	0	0 / 0	0 / 0	75 / 2	7 / 2	2 / 8	0g	0g	0%	35%	0%	0%
Nectarine 1 medium (140 g/5.0 oz)	60	5	0.5 / 1	0 / 0	250 / 7	15 / 5	2 / 8	11g	1g	8%	15%	0%	2%
Orange 1 medium (154 g/5.5 oz)	80	0	0 / 0	0 / 0	250 / 7	19 / 6	3 / 12	14g	1g	2%	130%	6%	0%
Peach 1 medium (147 g/5.3 oz)	60	0	0.5 / 1	0 / 0	230 / 7	15 / 5	2 / 8	13g	1g	6%	15%	0%	2%
Pear 1 medium (166 g/5.9 oz)	100	0	0 / 0	0 / 0	190 / 5	26 / 9	6 / 24	16g	1g	0%	10%	2%	0%
Pineapple 2 slices, 3" diameter, 3/4" thick (112 g/4 oz)	50	0	0 / 0	10 / 0	120 / 3	13 / 4	1 / 4	10g	1g	2%	50%	2%	2%
Plums 2 medium (151 g/5.4 oz)	70	0	0 / 0	0 / 0	230 / 7	19 / 6	2 / 8	16g	1g	8%	10%	0%	2%
Strawberries 8 medium (147g/5.3 oz)	50	0	0 / 0	0 / 0	170 / 5	11 / 4	2 / 8	8g	1g	0%	160%	2%	2%
Sweet Cherries 21 cherries; 1 cup (140 g/5.0 oz)	100	0	0 / 0	0 / 0	350 / 10	26 / 9	1 / 4	16g	1g	2%	15%	2%	2%
Tangerine 1 medium (109 g/3.9 oz)	50	0	0 / 0	0 / 0	160 / 5	13 / 4	2 / 8	9g	1g	6%	45%	4%	0%
Watermelon 1/18 medium melon; 2 cups diced pieces (280 g/10.0 oz)	80	0	0 / 0	0 / 0	270 / 8	21 / 7	1 / 4	20g	1g	30%	25%	2%	4%

Here are the nutrition facts for many kinds of raw fruit. Fruit is a great source of many different kinds of nutrients. Fruit also has very little, if any, fat and cholesterol, which can cause health problems.

RESEARCH PROJECT

Use magazines or print up photos from the Internet to make a chart of many different kinds of fruit. Arrange the pictures of fruit on a piece of cardboard in a "rainbow" as described in "Make Connections" in this chapter. Find at least 5 different fruits for each color. Label each color and explain how that color of fruit helps keep your body healthy.

TEXT-DEPENDENT QUESTIONS

1. List four vitamins and four kinds of minerals.

2. What are three kinds of carbohydrates?

3. How does this chapter say that candy and fruit are alike?

4. How are they different?

5. Explain what this chapter means when it says you should "eat the rainbow."

eat the apple. You'll get more vitamins along with the sugar when you eat fruit.

Your body also digests the sugar in fruit differently from how it handles candy. When you eat candy, your body digests all the sugar at once because candy is pretty much just sugar. You get a rush of energy and then a crash a little later on. The sugar you don't use up right away gets turned into fat and stored for later.

While fruit has some sugar, it also has lots of fiber. The fiber lets your body digest the sugar more slowly. You use it all up over a longer time, so you don't have to store extra sugar as fat. Plus, you don't get that crash in energy.

Fruits also contain smaller amounts of lots of other nutrients. All together, the nutrients in fruit keep your energy up and help your body work right.

THE POWER OF FRUITS

Eating fruits and vegetables is often lumped together into one category. Both kinds of food offer the same sorts of benefits, so it's important to eat both. But some people find eating fruits a little easier than eating vegetables, because they like the taste of fruit better than vegetables' taste.

Eating enough fruits and getting the nutrients inside will help protect you from getting serious diseases. Scientists have found that eating fruits may help protect people from serious illnesses like heart attacks. They also may protect against certain kinds of cancers like stomach cancer, lung cancer, and colon cancer. Some studies have even found that people who already have heart disease benefit from fruits. People with blocked arteries who exercised and ate lots of fruits and vegetables actually got rid of some of the blockage! Fruits may also help prevent some kinds of *diabetes*, *stroke*, *cataracts*, *obesity*, *asthma*, and *high blood pressure*.

That's not to say that if you eat fruit you'll never get sick—but you might have a better chance of avoiding serious illness if you always eat lots of fruit along with other healthy foods. Fruits do a lot of great stuff!

WORDS TO UNDERSTAND

diet: All the food you eat.
categories: Groups.
variety: A range of different things or choices.
allergies: Bad reactions from your body against something in your food or in the world around you.

Chapter 3

So Why Can't I Eat Only Fruit Every Day?

I f fruits are so great and you like them, you may be thinking: Why couldn't I just eat fruit and only fruit every day? Then you could forget about all the other foods you don't like.

But that's not the way a healthy diet works. While you should eat fruits every day, you shouldn't eat *only* fruit. The healthiest **diet** is a balanced one. Healthy eating means eating many different kinds of foods.

FOOD GROUPS

Fruits are just one of many types of food. While fruits are important, so are the other four **categories** of food we eat. These categories are called food groups.

Vegetables are one food group. Like fruits, vegetables come from plants that grow in the ground. There are lots of different kinds of vegetables, from lettuce and spinach to

The U.S. government suggests that at least half of the food you eat each day should be fruits and vegetables. Choosing fruits and vegetables over less-healthy foods (like soda, fast food, and candy) is a great way to stay in shape and feel good.

tomatoes to rutabagas and turnips. Vegetables have many of the same nutrients as fruits, plus a lot more. Vegetables can pack in nutrients like iron and vitamin B, among others.

Grains are another food group. Grains are the seeds of certain kinds of plants related to grass. Rice, wheat, barley, oats, and even corn are all considered grains. Whole grains are the best grains to eat. Grains have three different parts, each one containing nutrients. Refined grains like white rice have two of those parts—and their nutrients—taken out. Whole grains have all the parts and all the nutrients. Grains contain vitamin B, iron, magnesium, fiber, and more.

MAKE CONNECTIONS

What if you only ate fruit but added a multivitamin to your diet? Vitamins do give you an added boost of nutrients if you take them regularly. However, most doctors agree that vitamins just aren't as good as eating real food with nutrients. Your body doesn't absorb or use the nutrients in a pill quite the same way as it does with whole food. You're much better off eating a balanced diet rather than only your fruits and popping a vitamin.

Protein is a fourth food group. Lots of foods count as protein foods, like meat, eggs, beans (including tofu, which is made out of soybeans), and nuts.

Finally, the fifth food group is dairy. All dairy foods come from animal milk. Milk itself counts as a dairy food, and so do yogurt, cheese, and sour cream. Dairy foods are rich in vitamin D and calcium.

A BALANCED DIET

In general, people need to eat from each food group if they can. Eating from each food group helps you get a wide range of nutrients. This is called eating a balanced diet.

The word diet can mean two different things. A diet can be a way of eating that helps someone lose weight. Diet can also just mean the range of food someone eats normally, along with the amount someone eats. A healthy diet would include eating the right amount of food with lots of good nutrients. An unhealthy diet would include foods without many nutrients, and it might also include eating too much. A balanced diet refers to the second definition of the word diet.

Your goal is to get all the nutrients you need every day. You can only do that by eating a *variety* of foods. Imagine that you only ate oranges every day. You love oranges, and by themselves, oranges are very healthy. They have vitamin C. They also have sugar and fiber and a little potassium and calcium. Great! They don't have a lot of other nutrients, though. They don't have vitamin K or iron or fat or protein. Those are all nutrients you also really need to be healthy. So if you only ate oranges, you wouldn't be getting those nutrients at all. You'd probably get sick.

You'd get a few more nutrients if you ate fruits other than oranges but still ate only fruits. You'd get some vitamin A and some more potassium. You still wouldn't be getting nutrients that make up other food groups, like protein and iron. Eating just fruit isn't enough.

But fruits *are* part of a balanced diet. You wouldn't want to leave them out while eating the other food groups. Fruits are high in some nutrients that are harder to find in foods from other groups. That's why you need to eat some from all five food groups every day.

However, sometimes people can't eat from all five food groups. Many people have food *allergies* or they can't digest certain foods. Dairy is a good example—lots of people can't

Combining different kinds of food at each meal is a good way to make sure you're eating enough of each of the five food groups. Have a piece of fruit with your breakfast cereal every day to start your day with energy!

RESEARCH PROJECT

Certain diseases are caused by not getting enough of a particular nutrient. This is sometimes called a "deficiency." Use the Internet to search for 5 illnesses caused by a deficiency of some nutrient. Write down the names of these illnesses, explain what causes them, and list their symptoms.

TEXT-DEPENDENT QUESTIONS

1. List the five food groups.

2. What does this chapter say a "balanced diet" means?

3. List 5 nutrients this chapter says are in oranges.

4. Explain why you wouldn't be healthy if you ate only oranges every day.

5. List two foods besides meat that the chapter says contain protein.

digest dairy. Other people choose not to eat certain food groups for personal reasons. Vegetarians don't eat meat, and vegans don't eat meat or dairy.

People who have dietary restrictions have to pay a little more attention to the nutrients they're eating. Vegetarians have to make sure, for example, they're getting enough protein if they're not eating meat. Luckily, beans and nuts have plenty of protein in them. People who can't or don't eat dairy have to find other sources of calcium. Dark, leafy greens like kale and spinach have a lot of calcium, so they'll have to eat more of those.

WORDS TO UNDERSTAND

nutritionists: Scientists who study the food people eat and how it affects them.

Chapter 4

Putting Fruits on My Plate Every Day

Sure, you can eat fruits every day, but how do you know how much fruit you're supposed to eat? The United States Department of Agriculture (USDA) has made a guide to tell you just that. *Nutritionists* worked together to make the guide.

The USDA's guide is called MyPlate. You can use it as a tool to remind yourself to eat all five food groups, and to figure out how much of each food group you'll need to eat.

UNDERSTANDING MYPLATE

MyPlate looks like it sounds—like a plate. The plate is divided into four sections. In one half are two sections, one for fruit and one for vegetables. The section for vegetables is slightly bigger than the one for fruits. The other half of the plate is divided in half again between grains and protein. In the corner is a glass labeled dairy.

MAKE CONNECTIONS

Juice can count as fruit if it's 100 percent fruit juice. A lot of the juice in stores is mostly just sugar water, though. Check the label to see what percent fruit juice it is. First, look to see if the label says something like "10 percent fruit juice." Then you know most of it is sugar and water. The ingredient list on the label should also list only fruit juice and not lots of other ingredients. If the first ingredients are water and sugar or high fructose corn syrup (a kind of sugar), you're not drinking 100 percent fruit juice. Doctors mostly agree that drinking even 100 percent fruit juice is not as good as eating whole fruit. Juice can be part of a balanced diet, but be sure to eat more fruit than juice.

The size of each section gives you a clue as to how much of each food group you're supposed to eat. Imagine you're eating dinner. If you divided your plate into the five food groups, each one should fit into its section.

So one-quarter of your plate should be grains. One-quarter should be protein. A little more than one-quarter should be vegetables. And a little less than one-quarter should be fruit. Don't forget the glass of milk on the side!

Let's think about that in terms of a real meal. For dinner, you might have spaghetti with sauce. The sauce is homemade and is made out of tomatoes, onions, and peppers. There's also broccoli and chicken mixed in the pasta. On the side is a cup of fruit salad and a glass of milk.

If you separated out all the different food groups into different corners of your plate, it would look a lot like MyPlate. People don't always eat with their food groups separated, but you can imagine separating all your food out to see how much of one food group you're eating compared to others.

Every meal you eat may not look exactly like MyPlate. For example, you might not eat vegetables every day for breakfast. Does that mean your diet isn't balanced?

No. MyPlate makes the most sense if you think about following it over your whole day. For breakfast you might have oatmeal with a sliced banana and a glass of milk. You had some grains (the oatmeal), fruit, and dairy. You haven't had any protein or vegetables yet.

That's where lunch comes in. You eat a sandwich made with whole grain bread, turkey, lettuce, and tomatoes. You also have some carrot sticks and a cup of yogurt. By lunchtime, now you've had some vegetables, some more grains, some protein, and a little more dairy. You didn't eat fruit this meal, but you already got some today. You can have an apple for a snack later, so that you keep up with that food group.

By the end of the day, you want one-quarter of all the food you ate to have been protein. One-quarter should have been grains. A little more than a quarter should have been vegetables. A little less than a quarter should have been fruit. And you need some dairy, whether that's milk or another dairy food.

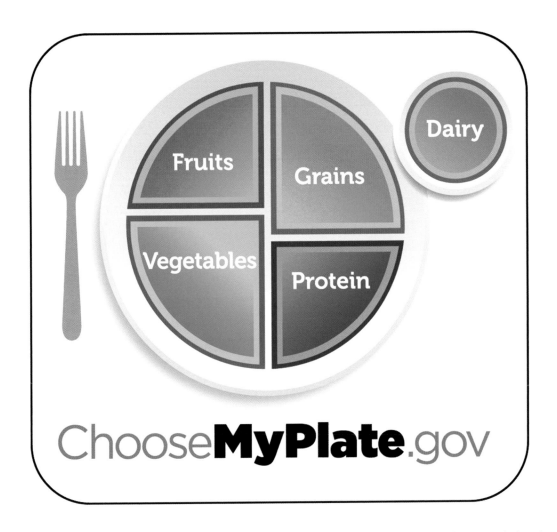

The USDA's MyPlate is designed to show how much of the food you eat should be from each food group. Whether you eat a lot or a little, about half of what you eat should be fruits and vegetables.

FOCUS ON FRUITS

The MyPlate website gives you a lot of information about the different food groups, including fruit. For example, it tells you just how much fruit you need to eat every day. Knowing how much to eat in relation to all the other food groups isn't enough.

Here is how much fruit MyPlate suggests you eat every day, based on your age and whether you're a boy or a girl:

- Children 2–3 years old: 1 cup
- Children 4–8 years old: 1 to 1.5 cups
- Girls 9–13 years old: 1.5 cups
- Boys 9–13 years old: 1.5 cups
- Girls 14–18 years old: 1.5 cups

How much is one cup of fruit?

Fruit	Serving size	How many cups?
Banana	1 large banana	1 cup of fruit
Gala apple	1 small gala apple	1 cup of fruit
Grapefruit	1 half of a medium grapefruit	1/2 cup of fruit
Grapes	About 50 grapes	1 1/2 cups of fruit
Mango	1 medium mango	1 cup of fruit
Orange	1 small orange	1/2 cup of fruit
Peach	1 large peach	1 cup of fruit
Plums	2 large plums	1 cup of fruit

ChooseMyPlate.gov has information about how much fruit you should be eating each day, including how much of your favorite fruit adds up to 1 cup. Keeping track of how much you eat is a great way to make sure you're eating enough fruit each day.

- Boys 14–18 years old: 2 cups
- Women 19–30 years old: 2 cups
- Men 19–30 years old: 2 cups
- Women 31–50 years old: 1.5 cups
- Men 31–50 years old: 2 cups
- Women 51+ years old: 1.5 cups
- Men 51+ years old: 2 cups

You can see that young people need less fruit. As people get older, they need more fruit, although older women past thirty also need a little less. Find where you fall on the list to figure out how much fruit you should eat each day.

MyPlate points out that these amounts are for people who are not very active (people

RESEARCH PROJECT

Draw 21 blank MyPlate charts that look like the ones made by the USDA. Each day for a week, fill in one of the charts with what you actually ate for that meal. At the end of the week, look back. Is your diet balanced? Why or why not? Is there something you should do to change how you eat to make your diet healthier?

TEXT-DEPENDENT QUESTIONS

1. According to MyPlate, how much fruit should you eat at every meal?

2. Using the list given in the text, how much fruit do you need to eat every day (based on how old you are and whether you're a boy or a girl)?

3. What does the text say about juice? How can you tell if the juice you're drinking is healthy? Is it as good for you as a piece of fruit?

who don't exercise a lot). If you are very active or you are an athlete, you'll probably need more fruit every day, and more food in general.

You're still missing a key piece of information, though—what does half a cup, a cup, or two cups of fruit look like?

One piece of whole fruit is generally a cup. So one apple, one orange, one banana, and one mango is a cup. One cup of 100 percent fruit juice also counts as a cup. One-half cup of dried fruit actually counts as a whole cup of fruit. Dried fruit has all the nutrients of fresh fruit, but the water has been taken out. If you picture dried fruit with the water put back in, you can see how a half a cup is closer to one cup of fresh fruit. A half-cup of fruit will be about the size of half your fist.

MyPlate gives you tips on what counts as the fruit food group and how much you should be getting every day. Then you'll need to figure out is just how to include enough fruits in your diet every day.

Chapter

5

Fast Foods, Snacks, and Fruit

Fruits are an anytime food! You can eat fruit for breakfast, lunch, and dinner. Fruits are also great for snacks. You can even include them in meals when you eat out, if you get a little creative.

FAST FOOD

When you think of fast food, you might not automatically think of fruit. A lot of fast foods are greasy hamburgers and fries and sugary sodas. That's true, but fast food can also include fruit.

A lot of fast food is pretty unhealthy. Fast food is unhealthy for three main reasons.

Fast food meals usually don't have a lot of good nutrients in them. Fruits, on the other hand, have plenty of good nutrients. Adding fruit to your fast food meal adds good nutrients.

Second, fast foods have too much of some nutrients. Sodium is one good example.

Nutrition facts

Serving size 1 cup (9 oz - 255g)
Servings per container 2

Amount per serving
Calories 485   **Calories from fat 220**

	% Daily Value*
Total fat 1 oz - 28 g	**32%**
Satured fat 0.5 oz - 14g	38%
Trans fat 0.2 oz - 6g	
Sodium 0.03 oz - 0.9g	**13%**
Total carbohydrate 1.5 oz - 42g	**11%**
Dietary fiber 0 oz - 0g	0%
Sugars 0.2 oz - 6g	
Protein 0.2 oz - 6g	
Vitamin A 5% **Calcium** 18%	
Vitamin C 3% **Iron** 6%	

* Percent Daily Value are based on a 2500 calorie diet. Your Daily Value may be higher or lower depending on your calorie need.

Limit these nutrients

Get enough of these nutrients

Quick Guide to % Daily Value:

5% or less is low

20% or more is high

Most foods in the United States have a nutrition facts label like this one. This helps you keep track of the nutrients each food has in it, and it makes it easy to make healthier choices.

People need sodium (another word for salt) in small amounts. A little bit of sodium keeps people healthy. Lots of sodium, however, is not healthy. Eating too much sodium over time can lead to heart disease and other health problems. Fast food often has too much sodium. It also has too much fat and too much sugar, both of which cause health problems when they're eaten in large amounts.

We call a food that has a lot of calories but not a lot of vitamins or minerals "empty calories." You need calories in your diet to live, but try to get them from foods high in vitamins and minerals!

Finally, fast foods are unhealthy because they have too many calories. Calories are how we measure the **energy** in food. A hamburger with 600 calories has a lot of energy. An apple with 60 calories has a little bit of energy. People need about 1,800 to 2,000 calories a day, depending on their age, sex, and how active they are. Eating more calories than that causes weight gain. Eating fewer causes weight loss. The problem with fast food is that it has lots and lots of calories and not many good nutrients. One fast food meal can pack in 1,000 calories! That's half of the calories you need in a day, but just in one meal. Too many fast food meals lead to weight gain, along with lots of other health problems.

Luckily, there are ways of making fast food meals healthier. Adding fruits to your fast food meal is one way to add in some nutrition. Fruit adds more good nutrients. Anytime you can add fruit to your diet, it's a good choice.

Many fast food restaurants are realizing that people want to eat healthier. They're adding more fruits to their menus to give people the choice to add some healthy food to their meal.

You'll have to search the menu carefully to find fruit, but it's often there! Some kids' meals these days include apple slices or other fruit choices. They also sometimes have a 100 percent fruit juice choice for a drink, instead of soda. Other choices include fruit salads, fruit parfaits with yogurt, smoothies with real fruit, and oatmeal with fruit.

If you have the choice between apples and french fries, for example, you should choose

Eating snacks throughout the day can keep your energy up and help you eat smaller meals. Make sure you're snacking on healthy foods like fruits and vegetables, though—not junk foods.

the apples most of the time. French fries are a food you should just eat once in a while. The more fruits you choose at a fast food restaurant, the better!

SNACKS

Snacks are where fruit really shines. Snacks are a great way to keep your energy up and get all five food groups during the day. Lots of people choose to eat fruit for a snack.

RESEARCH PROJECT

Use the Internet to come up with ideas for 5 new healthy snacks that you don't normally eat. Research what nutrients are in each of these snacks. Then make a shopping list for your parents. Ask them if they'd be willing to try out the new snacks. Explain to them what nutrients are in each snack, and why eating those nutrients will help you be healthier. If they agree to try the snacks, make sure you eat them!

TEXT-DEPENDENT QUESTIONS

1. What are the three things the text lists as the reasons why fast foods are often not very healthy?

2. What are calories? How are they connected to your weight?

3. List five ways you could order fruit at a fast-food restaurant.

4. Explain why junk foods don't make good snacks.

Let's say you've eaten toast and peanut butter for breakfast with a glass of milk. You had chicken and vegetable soup for lunch. So far, you had some pretty healthy foods and gotten some good nutrients.

You haven't had fruit yet, though. You can make sure you eat some fruit for the day with a snack.

Snacks also keep you going throughout the day. If you eat breakfast at 7:00 in the morning and don't eat lunch until 12:30, that's five and a half hours between meals! You might need some fuel to keep you going. The best fuel is healthy snacks, not junk food like chips and candy.

Junk food won't keep your energy up like healthier snacks will. Eating a candy bar might give you a short burst of energy because of the sugar. Then you'll crash and feel really tired. If you're looking for a sugary snack, fruits are a much better choice.

Here are some snack ideas that include fruits (and other healthy foods):

- apple slices with peanut butter
- a whole piece of fruit like an orange, peach, or banana
- a handful of dried fruits like raisins or apricots
- a smoothie with bananas or berries and no added sugar
- fruit salad
- fruit kabobs: cut up pineapple, peaches, apples, grapes, berries, or your other favorite fruits skewered onto a toothpick or shish kabob stick
- frozen juice bars (make sure they're 100 percent fruit juice)
- unsweetened applesauce

Use your imagination and your favorite fruits to come up with new snacks. You can also use snack time to try new fruits you've never had before. Never tried a kiwi? Try some for a snack. What about star fruit? Be adventurous. You may discover a new favorite food.

WORDS TO UNDERSTAND

obese: Overweight by more than is healthy.

absorb: To take in.

reduce: To lessen.

genes: The basic building blocks that make up who we are, passed on to us from each of our parents.

Chapter 6

The Big Picture

As you get older, you'll start to have more and more control over what you eat. The choices you make will directly affect your health. Choosing to eat healthy foods makes a big difference in your life both today and in the future.

HEALTH FOR TODAY

Eating healthy foods like fruits has a lot to do with how you feel and how healthy you are right now. Eating too many unhealthy foods can make you feel sick and tired. Healthy foods help keep you feeling healthy and happy.

Pay attention to how you feel after you eat. You'll start to notice that you feel different after eating different kinds of food. You might feel like you have tons of energy and are ready for anything after you eat a lot of fruits and vegetables. Or you might feel gross and tired after you eat a lot of junk food or fast food.

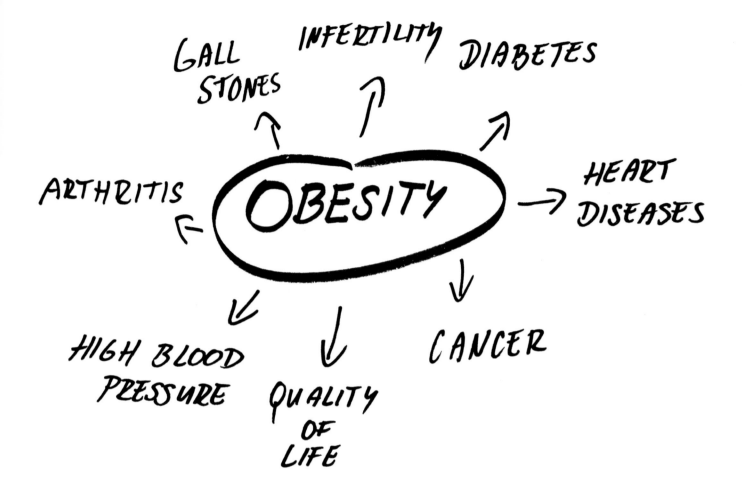

Obesity increases the chances that you'll have many other health conditions. Eating healthy and avoiding obesity can help you live a long, healthy life.

Healthy foods tend to keep your energy steady. One of the main purposes of eating is to keep our bodies going. Food allows us to go to school, do sports, hang out with friends, and everything else we do in life.

After you eat healthy foods, you should feel ready to keep going with your day. Unhealthy foods, on the other hand, often make people feel really tired and ready to fall asleep. Or they give people a short burst of energy and then lead to a crash and a huge drop in energy. Healthy foods give you steady energy so that you can keep going at your best until the next meal.

Eating a balanced diet also helps prevent you from getting sick. Healthy foods can boost the immune system, the body system that fights bacteria and viruses that make us sick. That doesn't mean you won't ever get a cold or the flu again if you eat healthier, but you may get sick less often.

A balanced, healthy diet also keeps your weight healthy. A healthy weight doesn't have anything to do with looking good or being a good person. It has everything to do with not getting seriously sick. Everyone has a different healthy weight depending on his body. We don't all have to be the same weight to be healthy. But a healthy weight is important for everyone. Being overweight or **obese** can lead to problems in the future, but it can also cause problems while you're still young. For example, eating unhealthy foods and weighing too much can lead to diabetes.

Diabetes is a disease that changes how the body deals with sugar. In a healthy person, a substance called insulin helps the body **absorb** and use sugar. Bodies of people with diabetes don't make enough insulin. Diabetes can lead to kidney problems, eye problems, foot problems, and more.

In the past, young people generally only developed one kind of diabetes, called type I diabetes. That type doesn't really have anything to do with diet or weight. Type II diabetes is the variety that is tied to unhealthy foods and weight. Mostly adults got type II diabetes in the past. However, today people are eating such unhealthy diets that more and more young people are getting type II diabetes. Type II diabetes is no longer just an adult disease. Kids and teens who develop it have to live with the disease for the rest of their lives.

Unhealthy weight can also mean weighing too little, not only weighing too much. Some young people feel pressure to be thin. They don't eat enough food. Other people just forget to eat during their busy lives. Healthy eating is all about eating enough food too. All human beings need enough food for their bodies to work right and to get through the day.

Eating too little leads to low energy and trouble getting through the day. People who are underweight may not be getting all the nutrients they need, so their bodies aren't working right. They also may get sick more often than people with healthier diets.

When you pay attention to how food makes you feel, you can start really understanding what it means to eat healthy. And you'll have reasons to eat healthy right now, because you feel better and you have more energy!

HEALTH FOR TOMORROW

It's easier to think about how healthy you are right now. Why worry about your health in the future? You may feel as though the future is far away!

Getting your family involved in choosing healthy foods can help you stick with healthy eating. If you don't think you're eating enough fruits and vegetables, talk to your parents about bringing more balance to your family diet.

But you'll get older before you know it. Pretty soon, you'll realize that all the choices you made as a young person really shape your health as an adult.

Eating healthy is one of the single best decisions you can make in your life right now. You'll **reduce** your risk for all kinds of health problems later on.

The list of diseases caused at least partly by an unhealthy diet is long. The list includes stroke, diabetes, heart attack, blocked arteries, osteoporosis (a bone disease), asthma, liver and kidney problems, and even some kinds of cancer.

Eating healthy doesn't mean you'll never get cancer or have a heart problem. Other things like your **genes** and how much you exercise have a lot to do with disease. But you

A lot of the time, healthy eating is about making good habits. If you're in the habit of snacking on fruit, you'll be healthier than if you always eat chips or cookies.

RESEARCH PROJECT

Make a list of five things you would like to do when you grow up. Then think about how good health is related to each thing. Use the Internet or library if you need to find out more, or ask your teachers and parents for their ideas. If you were overweight, had heart disease, or got diabetes or some other disease related to poor nutrition, how would that affect your chances of doing the things you hope to do? List five choices you can make today that will help you protect your dreams for the future.

are reducing your chances for getting those serious diseases. There's no reason not to eat healthy!

Fruits and other healthy foods will help keep you healthy now and in the future. Fruits are part of a balanced diet. They give you all sorts of nutrients that keep your body working right. They are a key part of eating healthy. Besides, adding fruit to your diet is easy and fun!

Find Out More

ONLINE

Fresh for Kids
www.freshforkids.com.au/fruit_pages/fruit.html

Fruits and Veggies More Matters
www.fruitsandveggiesmorematters.org/why-fruits-veggies

KidsHealth: Nutrition and Fitness Center
kidshealth.org/kid/nutrition

MyPlate
www.choosemyplate.gov

Super Healthy Kids: Fruit Recipes
www.superhealthykids.com/healthy-kids-recipes/category/fruit-recipes.php

IN BOOKS

Bickerstaff, Linda. *Nutrition Sense: Counting Calories, Figuring Out Fats, and Eating Balanced Meals.* New York: Rosen Publishing, 2008.

Cohen, Marina. *Why We Need Vitamins.* New York: Crabtree Publishing, 2011.

Kalnins, Daina. *YUM: Your Ultimate Manual for Good Nutrition.* Montreal, Qc., Canada: Lobster Press, 2008.

Martineau, Susan and Hel James. *Fruits and Vegetables.* North Mankato, Minn.: Smart Apple Media, 2009.

Schuh, Mari. *Fruits on MyPlate.* North Mankato, Minn.: Capstone Press, 2012.

Series Glossary of Key Terms

Carbohydrates: The types of molecules in food that we get most of our energy from. Foods like sugars and grains are especially high in carbohydrates.

Dairy: Milk or foods that are made from milk.

Diabetes: A disease where the body can't use sugar to produce energy correctly.

Diet: All the foods and nutrients that you normally eat.

Energy: The power stored in food that lets your body move around and carry out other body functions.

Farm: A place where plants and animals are grown and raised to produce food.

Fast food: Food designed to be ready for the customer as fast as possible. Usually it's more expensive and less healthy than fresh food, but it is very convenient.

Fiber: Tough parts of plant foods that your body can't digest. Fiber helps your digestive system function normally.

Fruits: A food group that includes the edible parts of plants that contain the seeds. They are often colorful and have a sweet flavor.

Grains: The seeds of various kinds of grass plant. Grains include rice, wheat, corn, and many others. They are high in carbohydrates and fiber, and can be stored for a long time.

Harvest: The process of or time when crops are gathered.

Local foods: Foods that are grown close to where they are eaten, so they don't have to be transported very far.

Minerals: Materials found naturally in metals or rocks. Our bodies need certain minerals in very small quantities.

Nutrients: Any part of food that our body uses in some way to survive and stay healthy.

Obesity: A state of being so overweight that it's bad for your health.

Organic: A way of producing food in which no genetic modifications, harmful pesticides, or hormones can be used.

Protein: The chemical parts of food that your body uses to build muscles and perform certain body processes. If your body runs out of carbohydrates and fat, it will start using protein for energy.

Vegetables: Plant foods that are usually made of the flower, stem, leaf, or root of a plant. They are usually high in fiber and certain nutrients.

Vitamins: Certain kinds of molecules that your body cannot produce. Instead, you need to get them in your diet to stay healthy.

Index

About the Author & Consultant

Rosa Waters lives in New York State. She has worked as a writer for several years, producing works on health, history, and other topics.

Dr. Lisa Prock is a developmental behavioral pediatrician at Children's Hospital (Boston) and Harvard Medical School. She attended college at the University of Chicago, medical school at Columbia University, and received a master's degree in public health from the Harvard School of Public Health. Board-certified in general pediatrics and developmental behavioral pediatrics, she currently is Clinical Director of Developmental and Behavioral Pediatrics and Consultant to the Walker School, a residential school serving children in foster care. Dr. Prock has combined her clinical interests in child development and international health with advocacy for children in medical, residential, and educational settings since 1991. She has worked in Cambodia teaching pediatrics and studying tuberculosis epidemiology; and in Eastern Europe visiting children with severe neurodevelopmental challenges in orphanages. She has co-authored numerous original publications and articles for families. She is a also nonprofit board member for organizations and has received numerous local and national awards for her work with children and families.

Picture Credits